My first numbers

PRICE STERN SLOAN

PRICE STERN SLOAN LIMITED, NORTHAMPTON, ENGLAND

The fun way to bring learning to life

This book is part of the **Questron** system, which offers children a unique aid to learning and endless hours of challenging entertainment.

The **Questron** Electronic Answer Wand uses a microchip to sense correct and incorrect answers with ''right'' or ''wrong'' sounds and lights. Victory sounds and lights reward the user when particular sets of questions or games are completed. Powered by a nine-volt alkaline battery, which is activated only when the wand is pressed on a page, **Questron** should have an exceptionally long life. The **Questron** Electronic Answer Wand can be used with any book in the **Questron** series.

A note to parents...

With **Questron**, right or wrong answers are indicated instantly and can be tried over and over again to reinforce learning and improve skills. Children need not be restricted to the books designated for their age group, as interests and rates of development vary widely. Also, within many of the books, certain pages are designed for the older end of the age group and will provide a stimulating challenge to younger children.

Many activities are designed at different levels. For example, the child can select an answer by recognizing a letter or by reading an entire word. The activities for pre-readers and early readers are intended to be used with parental assistance. Interaction with parents or older children will stimulate the learning experience.

Printed in Great Britain by
Purnell Book Production Limited
Member of the BPCC Group

How to start
Questron®

Hold **Questron**
at this angle and press the
activator button firmly on the page.

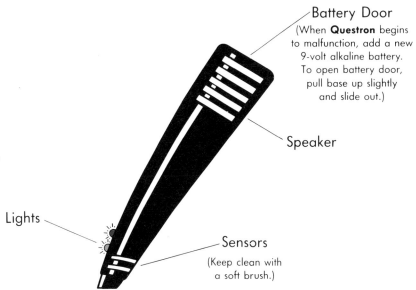

Battery Door
(When **Questron** begins
to malfunction, add a new
9-volt alkaline battery.
To open battery door,
pull base up slightly
and slide out.)

Speaker

Lights

Sensors
(Keep clean with
a soft brush.)

How to use
Questron®

Press

Press **Questron** firmly on
the shape below, then lift it off.

Track

Press **Questron** down on "Start" and keep it
pressed down as you move to "Finish".

Start   Finish

Right and wrong with
Questron®

Press **Questron**
on the square.

See the green light and
hear the sound. This
green light and sound
say "You are correct".

Press **Questron**
on the triangle.

The red light and sound
say "Try again". Lift
Questron off the page and
wait for the sound to stop.

Press **Questron**
on the circle.

Hear the victory sound.
Don't be dazzled
by the flashing lights.
You deserve them.

1

LOOK AT THE PICTURES.
FIND A PICTURE OF 1 ANIMAL.
PRESS THE ANIMAL WITH
QUESTRON. FIND ANOTHER
PICTURE OF 1 ANIMAL.

4

How Many?

MATCH THE PICTURE WITH THE NUMBERS. PRESS THE COLOURED SQUARES BELOW THE NUMBER THAT IS CORRECT.

1	2	3	4	5

1	2	3	4	5

1	2	3	4	5

1	2	3	4	5

2

TRACE **QUESTRON** AROUND THE NUMBER 2. THIS IS A GOOD WAY TO GET TO KNOW THE SHAPE OF A NUMBER.

LOOK FOR 2 OF A KIND. PRESS THEM BOTH WITH **QUESTRON**. FIND ANOTHER 2 OF A KIND.

NUMBER HUNT

TRACK **QUESTRON** ON THE STREETS. DRIVE UP TO EVERY BUILDING THAT HAS A NUMBER 1 ON IT. WHEN YOU HEAR THE VICTORY SOUND TAKE **QUESTRON** OFF THE PAGE BEFORE YOU BEGIN AGAIN.

Number Race

TRACK **QUESTRON** ON THE WINDING ROAD. MAKE SURE YOU TRAVEL OVER THE NUMBERS THAT MATCH THE SUMS.

1+1

START

2

3

2+1

1

3

2+2

3

4

3+1

4

FINISH

5

8

Number Sums

I CAN DO ADDITION PROBLEMS. CAN YOU?

PRESS **QUESTRON** ON THE COLOURED CIRCLE WITH THE NUMBER THAT YOU THINK IS CORRECT.

1 + 1 = ?	1	2	3	4
1 + 2 = ?	1	2	3	4
2 + 2 = ?	1	2	3	4
2 + 1 = ?	1	2	3	4
1 + 3 = ?	5	9	7	4
2 + 3 = ?	3	5	2	7

9

3

IF YOU LIKE MY NUMBERS PRESS MY BLACK BUTTON.

LOOK FOR 3 OF A KIND. PRESS **QUESTRON** ON EACH OF THE 3. LOOK FOR ANOTHER 3 OF A KIND.

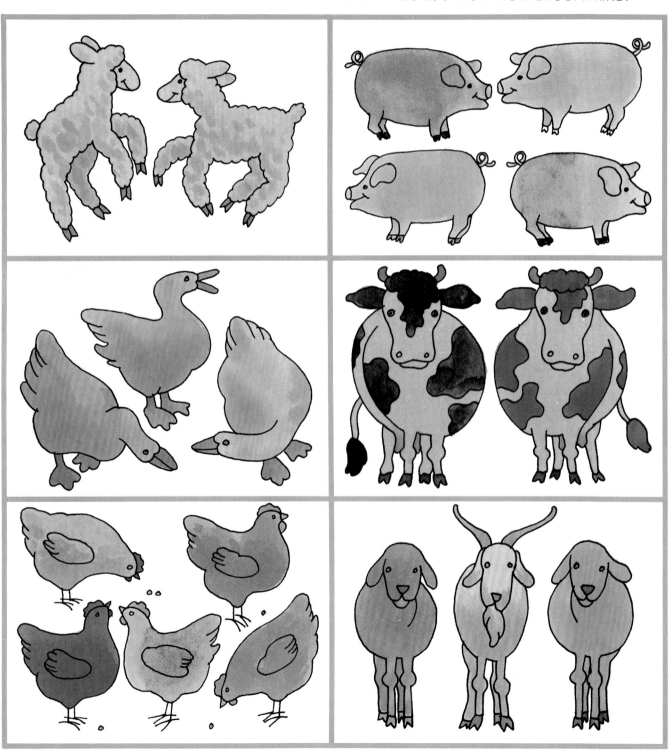

How Many?

HOW MANY OBJECTS ARE THERE? PRESS THE COLOURED SQUARES BELOW THE NUMBERS.

1	2	3	4	5

1	2	3	4	5

1	2	3	4	5

1	2	3	4	5

11

4

LOOK FOR 4 OF A KIND. PRESS **QUESTRON** ON EACH OF THE 4. LOOK FOR ANOTHER 4.

Which is the Smallest?

PRESS **QUESTRON** ON THE SMALLEST OBJECTS.

Number Fun

HOW MANY OBJECTS ARE THERE? PRESS THE COLOURED SQUARES BELOW THE NUMBERS WITH **QUESTRON**.

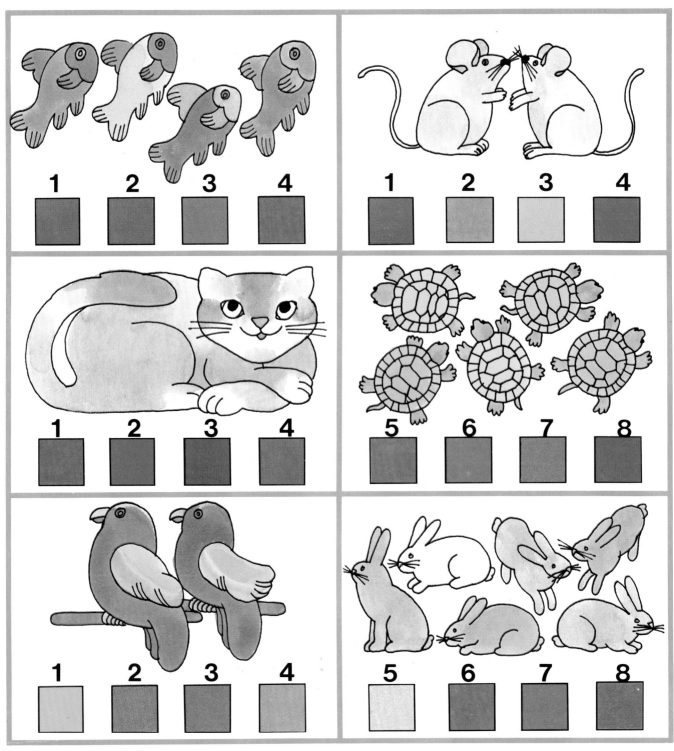

14

Nursery Rhyme Number Quiz

PRESS THE NUMBER IN THE COLOURED CIRCLE THAT YOU THINK IS CORRECT WITH **QUESTRON**.

Engine, engine
    Number
Going down
    Chicago Line

2   3   9

(**HINT**: WHAT NUMBER RHYMES WITH 'LINE'?)

Hickory, dickory, dock.
    The mouse ran up
the clock.
    The clock struck

4   2   1   3

The mouse ran down,
Hickory, dickory, dock.

(**HINT**: THE NUMBER DOES NOT RHYME WITH 'DOWN' BUT IT DOES RHYME WITH 'FUN'.)

5

I LIKE THE NUMBER 5.
DO YOU?

LOOK FOR 5 OF A KIND. PRESS **QUESTRON** ON EACH OF THE 5. LOOK FOR ANOTHER 5 OF A KIND.

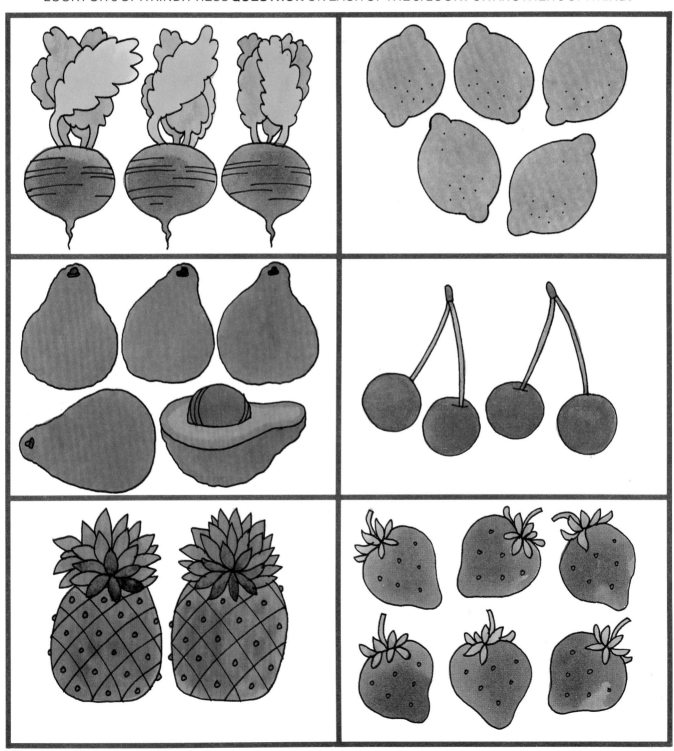

How Many?

1	2	3	4	5

1	2	3	4	5

1	2	3	4	5

1	2	3	4	5

17

6

CAN YOU FIND A
FLOWER IN YOUR
HOME OR SCHOOL
THAT HAS 6 PETALS?

LOOK FOR 6 OF A KIND. PRESS **QUESTRON** ON EACH OF THE 6. LOOK FOR ANOTHER 6 OF A KIND.

Number
Maze
Rockets

TRACK THE NUMBERS FROM 1 TO 5
FOR THE FIRST TWO ROCKETS AND FROM
1 TO 9 FOR THE THIRD ROCKET.

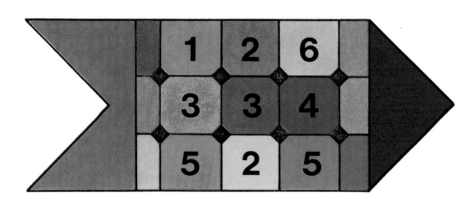

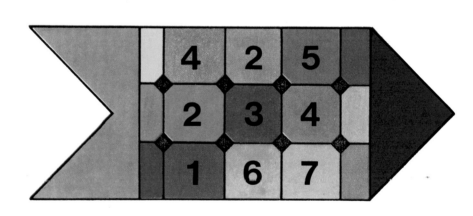

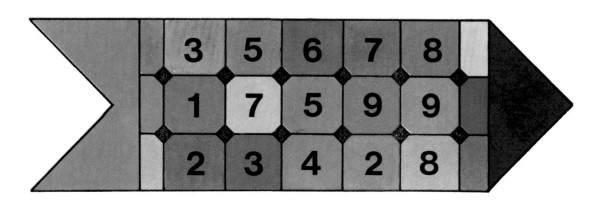

How Many Sides?

HOW MANY SIDES DO THE SHAPES HAVE? PRESS **QUESTRON** ON THE COLOURED SQUARES BELOW THE NUMBERS TO FIND OUT.

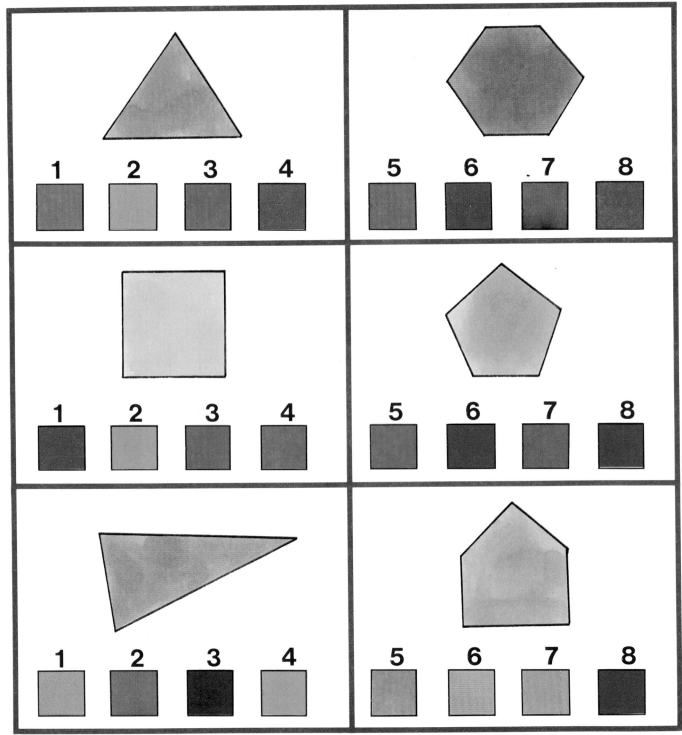

20

What Comes First?

PRESS THE COLOURED SQUARE IN THE PICTURE THAT SHOWS WHAT HAPPENED FIRST.

7

LOOK FOR 7 OF A KIND. PRESS **QUESTRON** ON EACH OF THE 7. LOOK FOR ANOTHER 7 OF A KIND.

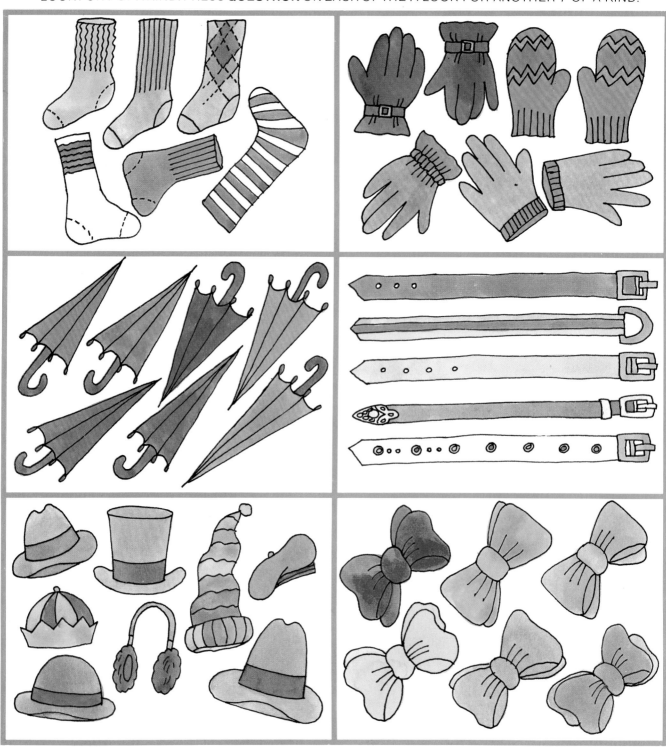

22

How Many?

5	6	7	8	9

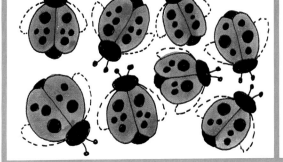

5	6	7	8	9

5	6	7	8	9

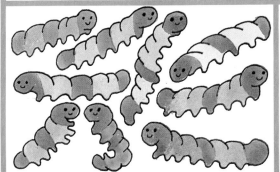

5	6	7	8	9

LOOK FOR 8 OF A KIND. PRESS **QUESTRON** ON EACH OF THE 8. LOOK FOR ANOTHER 8 OF A KIND.

SUNKEN TREASURE

FIND AND TRACK THE PATH THROUGH
THIS MAZE FROM THE SHIP TO THE
TREASURE.

Start

How Many?

ARE YOU HAVING FUN WITH NUMBERS?

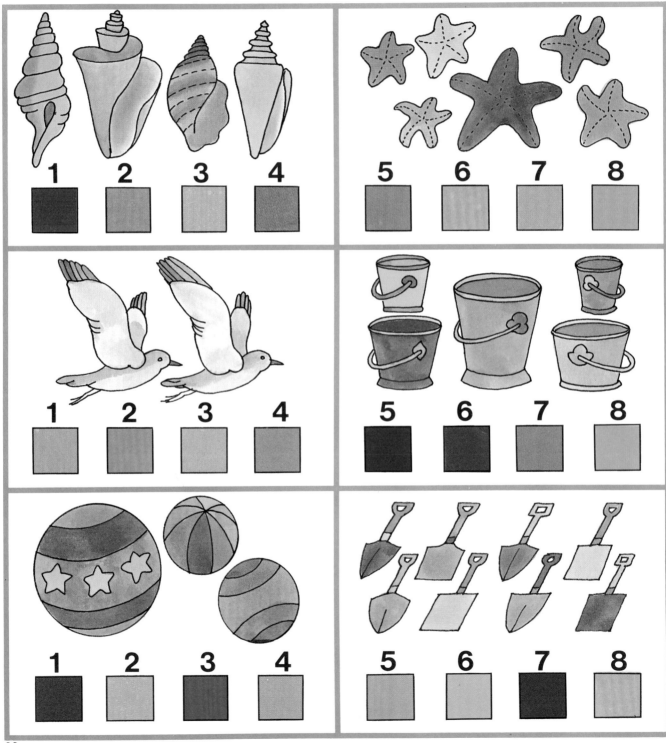

Number Quiz

PRESS THE COLOURED CIRCLE THAT CONTAINS THE CORRECT NUMBER.

How many bags of wool did "Baa, baa black sheep" have?

How many wheels on a car?

How many birthdays do you have a year?

How many letters are there in the word, **"QUESTRON"**?

How many legs does an octopus have?

9

LOOK FOR 9 OF A KIND. PRESS **QUESTRON** ON EACH OF THE 9. LOOK FOR ANOTHER 9 OF A KIND.

How Many?

CAN YOU DO THIS BY YOURSELF?

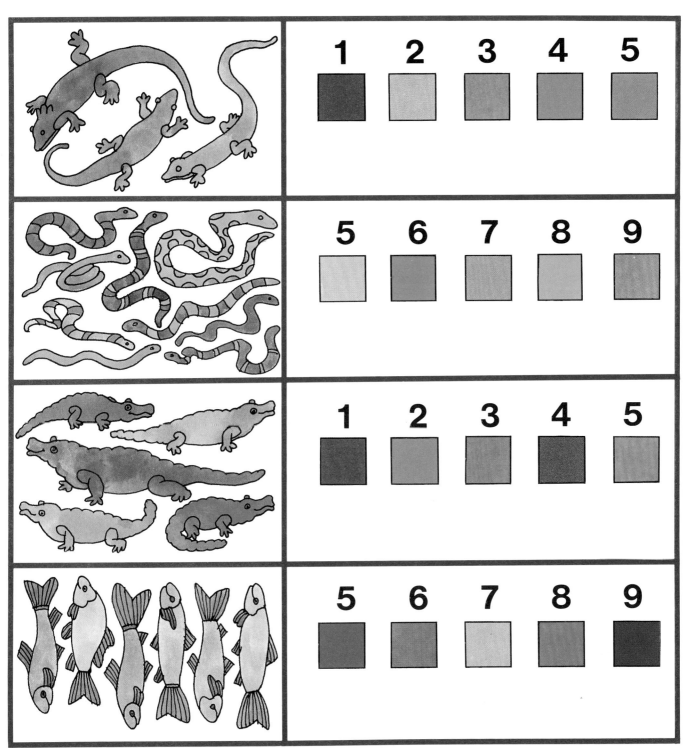

10

LOOK FOR 10 OF A KIND. PRESS **QUESTRON** ON EACH OF THE 10. LOOK FOR ANOTHER 10 OF A KIND.

Nursery Rhyme
Number Quiz

Rub a dub dub

(2)   (3)   (4)   (6)

Men in a tub.

The butcher, the baker,

The candlestick maker.

(5)   (4)   (3)   (2)

Little dicky birds,

Sitting on a wall,

One named Peter,

The other named Paul.

Another exciting children's series
Look, listen and join in the fun with

The Wee Sing range of cassettes and activity books are compiled by experienced preschool and early school teachers. The tapes include songs, games and rhymes. The books have the musical notes of the melody lines, so that children can have fun, sing along – and learn, too!

The Wee Sing and Colour series adds yet another dimension. The books not only contain the complete lyrics of the songs and rhymes – they also have line drawings of favourite characters to colour.

Wee Sing provides an hour of entertainment and music, and a songbook with no less than 64 pages. **Wee Sing and Colour** gives you some 30 minutes of songs, games and rhymes and a 48-page colouring book.

Wee Sing – early learning made fun.

Wee Sing

Children's songs and fingerplays
Rhymes for play
Nursery rhymes and lullabies
Silly songs

Wee Sing & Colour

Children's songs and fingerplays
Musical games and rhymes
Christmas songs

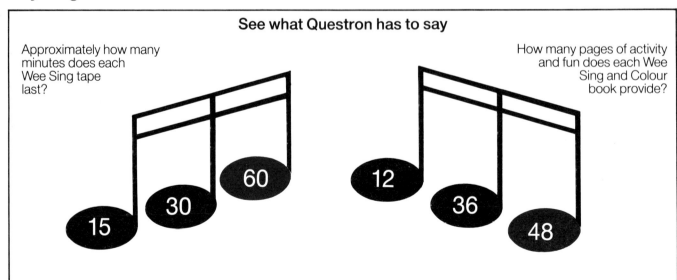

See what Questron has to say

Approximately how many minutes does each Wee Sing tape last?

15 30 60

How many pages of activity and fun does each Wee Sing and Colour book provide?

12 36 48

Another new product range from PSS – if you have difficulty in obtaining Wee Sing from your local stockist, please contact Price Stern Sloan Limited, John Clare House, The Avenue, Northampton NN1 5BT. Telephone (0604) 230344.